Just for today lord...

To: _____

From: _____

Date: _____

Rose Black

Just for Today Lord...

101 Inspirational Keepsake Messages that are both Entertaining & Thought Provoking

RIBlack Enterprises
St. Clair Shores, MI

Copyright © 2006 RIBlack Enterprises
ISBN: 978-0-9789849-0-8
Printed in the USA

Preface

As a person who continuously seeks inspiration from a higher power, Rose was motivated to write

"Just for Today Lord".

Just for today lord...

I will begin my day with a smile on my face
and a song in my heart.

Inspirational Message 1

Just for today lord...

I will start my journey knowing that you are
by my side every step of the way.

Inspirational Message 2

Just for today lord...

I will not make mountains out of mole hills, and if they do become mountains give me the strength to climb them, one at a time.

Inspirational Message 3

Just for today lord...

I will forget my problems and help someone who has greater needs than I do.

Inspirational Message 4

Just for today lord...

Let me live today as if there were no tomorrow.

Inspirational Message 5

Just for today lord...

Let your "Son" shine thru me all day.

Inspirational Message 6

Just for today lord...

Help me to remember that the world does not revolve around me.

Inspirational Message 7

Just for today lord...

I will try not to sweat the small stuff.

Inspirational Message 8

Just for today lord...

Lead me where you want me to go and make your presence known to whomever I meet.

Inspirational Message 9

Just for today lord...

Help me to remember that you are bigger than I am.

Inspirational Message 10

Just for today lord...

Help me to remember that with you by my side nothing is impossible.

Inspirational Message 11

Just for today lord...

I will do something that will make "You" smile.

Inspirational Message 12

Just for today lord...

Help me to make you my number one priority.

Just for today lord...

Help me not to complain about what I don't have but be thankful for what I do have.

Inspirational Message 14

Just for today lord...

I will try not to put both feet in my mouth because I do need one leg to stand on.

Inspirational Message 15

Just for today lord...

Help me refrain from judging the people I meet.

Just for today lord...

Though everyone I meet today may not meet
my expectations please help me to show
kindness & patience toward them.

Inspirational Message 17

Just for today lord...

I will put you first and foremost in everything I do, knowing that if I do that you will give me the strength to handle whatever comes my way.

Inspirational Message 18

Just for today lord...

I have chosen to serve only you in hopes that my actions will be obvious and contagious.

Inspirational Message 19

Just for today lord...

Make me smile and be thankful for all the things you have given me.

Inspirational Message 20

Just for today lord...

Let me be the kind of person that you would want me to be.

Inspirational Message 21

Just for today lord...

I will make an effort to be kind to everyone I meet.

Inspirational Message 22

Just for today lord...

Make me smile in the face of adversity knowing that you are my strength and my refuge.

Just for today lord...

Take me by the hand and walk with me wherever we go.

Just for today lord...

Help me not to be envious of other people—but just be thankful for who I am.

Just for today lord...

I want to thank you for my family because they are such an important part of who I am.

Just for today lord...

Help me to understand that my world should revolve around you and that your world doesn't revolve around me.

Inspirational Message 27

Just for today lord...

I will show at least one act of kindness toward another person.

Inspirational Message 28

Just for today lord...

Please protect me from harm wherever I go and whatever I do.

Inspirational Message 29

Just for today lord...

Make your face smile upon me and be gracious to me for you are the light that shines through me.

Inspirational Message 30

Just for today lord...

Help me to run faster and jump higher than I did yesterday.

Inspirational Message 31

Just for today lord...

Help me to have patience with those
that I encounter that cannot think or act
as fast as I think they should.

Inspirational Message 32

Just for today lord...

Put me in someone else's shoes so that I may understand their pain.

Inspirational Message 33

Just for today lord...

Let me give back one one-hundredth of what you have given me.

Just for today lord...

Let me not compare myself to anyone else because it is our uniqueness that make each one of us special.

Inspirational Message 35

Just for today lord...

Let me share with others the kindness
that you have shown me.

Inspirational Message 36

Just for today lord...

I will smile at least once.

Inspirational Message 37

Just for today lord...

I will not pass up the opportunity to help at least one person in need.

Inspirational Message 38

Just for today lord...

I will call someone I have not spoke to in years, just to say hi.

Inspirational Message 39

Just for today lord...

With your help, I will make peace with a parent, sibling, child, friend, or adversary.

Inspirational Message 40

Just for today lord...

With your help I will be at peace with who I am.

Inspirational Message 41

Just for today lord...

I will follow your lead in thought, word, and deed.

Inspirational Message 42

Just for today lord...

I will go in the direction you take me.

Inspirational Message 43

Just for today lord...

Help me to remember that without you I am nothing.

Inspirational Message 44

Just for today lord...

I will start my journey with you as my inspiration for all I do.

Inspirational Message 45

Just for today lord...

I know that today may not be my best day, but I will live knowing tomorrow will be a better day.

Inspirational Message 46

Just for today lord...

I will continue to dream knowing that without dreams we are nothing, so I will live my dreams.

Inspirational Message 47

Just for today lord...

I will take time to "Stop and smell the Roses".

Inspirational Message 48

Just for today lord...

I will take a moment to tell those that I love, that I love them.

Inspirational Message 49

Just for today lord...

I will not forget to thank those who have given me so much.

Inspirational Message 50

Just for today lord...

I will be so busy concentrating on my own life that I will not have time to criticize others.

Inspirational Message 51

Just for today lord...

I will seize the moment, fore I may never get the opportunity again.

Inspirational Message 52

Just for today lord...

I will pray for the people around the world that we may all unite in world peace.

Inspirational Message 53

Just for today lord...

I will ask you not to leave me alone, but to bestow on me your blessings and protection.

Inspirational Message 54

Just for today lord...

I will let my conscience be my guide in whatever I do.

Inspirational Message 55

Just for today lord...

Though I am not worthy, please forgive me for all of my short comings—for I am truly sorry.

Inspirational Message 56

Just for today lord...

I will listen closely to my inner voice.

Inspirational Message 57

Just for today lord...

I will be more concerned with what you think of me rather than what other people think of me.

Inspirational Message 58

Just for today lord...

I will be honest with myself and others.

Inspirational Message 59

Just for today lord...

I will laugh at my own faults and inadequacies.

Inspirational Message 60

Just for today lord...

I will try not to be so perfect that I cannot enjoy the day.

Inspirational Message 61

Just for today lord...

I will laugh with others and not at them.

Inspirational Message 62

Just for today lord...

With your help I know I will be able to handle whatever comes my way.

Inspirational Message 63

Just for today lord...

Help me to clear my mind and give all my thoughts to you.

Inspirational Message 64

Just for today lord...

Let my integrity be my guide.

Inspirational Message 65

Just for today lord...

Let my heart rejoice knowing that you are my salvation.

Inspirational Message 66

Just for today lord...

Let your face shine upon me and be
gracious unto me.

Inspirational Message 67

Just for today lord...

Let me start my day with a prayer.

Inspirational Message 68

Just for today lord...

Let my guardian angel spread it's wings over me to protect me.

Inspirational Message 69

Just for today lord...

Help me to make my dreams become a reality.

Inspirational Message 70

Just for today lord...

Help me to be "On-time" to wherever it is that I have to be.

Inspirational Message 71

Just for today lord...

Help me to "Slow down" so as to not get ahead of myself.

Just for today lord...

Help me to share my knowledge with those around me.

Inspirational Message 73

Just for today lord...

Help me to listen to others before I speak.

Inspirational Message 74

Just for today lord...

Help me to remember that life is not always about me.

Inspirational Message 75

Just for today lord...

Let me see your "Son" through the darkest cloud.

Inspirational Message 76

Just for today lord...

Help me to find the silver lining in every cloud.

Inspirational Message 77

Just for today lord...

Help me to surround myself with people who inspire me.

Inspirational Message 78

Just for today lord...

Help me to inspire just one person to fulfill their dreams.

Inspirational Message 79

Just for today lord...

Let my kindness be contagious.

Inspirational Message 80

Just for today lord...

Let my smile brighten someone's day.

Inspirational Message 81

Just for today lord...

Let me speak only kind words to those whom I meet.

Inspirational Message82

Just for today lord...

The devil will not get the best of me.

Inspirational Message83

Just for today lord...

I will not be the person who says: "It cannot be done".

Inspirational Message 84

Just for today lord...

Give me the strength to help others who are less fortunate than I.

Inspirational Message 85

Just for today lord...

I will not spend time doing things that do not have to be done at all.

Inspirational Message 86

Just for today lord...

I will tell the truth—knowing that I will not have to remember what I have said.

Inspirational Message 87

Just for today lord...

I will go one step beyond where people expect me to go.

Inspirational Message 88

Just for today lord...

I will live my dream.

Inspirational Message 89

Just for today lord...

I will not burn the bridges that some day
I may need to cross.

Inspirational Message 90

Just for today lord...

I will not fear the unknown.

Inspirational Message 91

Just for today lord...

I will not be so afraid to fail that I miss a "Golden Opportunity".

Inspirational Message 92

Just for today lord...

I will not use the terms: "Could have done", "Might have done", or "Should have done", I will just do it.

Inspirational Message 93

Just for today lord...

I will live in the present—not in the past or the future.

Inspirational Message 94

Just for today lord...

I will take responsibility for all of my actions.

Inspirational Message 95

Just for today lord...

I will not blame others for my misfortune.

Inspirational Message 96

Just for today lord...

I will learn to accept the situations in life that I cannot change and change the things I can.

Inspirational Message 97

Just for today lord...

I will not give up on anything.

Inspirational Message 98

Just for today lord...

I will take the time to listen to others before I speak.

Inspirational Message 99

Just for today lord...

I will be persistent in what I do—
therefore I will become a winner.

Inspirational Message 100

Just for today lord...

I will live...
"JUST FOR TODAY".

Inspirational Message 101

Notes

Notes